Praying the Name of
Jesus

Robert V. Dodd

THE UPPER ROOM
Nashville, Tennessee

Book Design: Harriette Bateman
Cover Transparency: Charles L. Tucker
First Printing: May, 1985 (3)
Library of Congress Catalog Number: 84-052228
ISBN 0-8358-0514-X

Printed in the United States of America

For all the people
who have helped me on my spiritual journey,
whose names are too numerous to mention
—and especially for my wife Ann.

Contents

Foreword

Robert V. Dodd has opened a way for those who desire to deepen their experiences in prayer. All Christians offer prayers. Most feel inadequate, however, and struggle to offer the "effectual, fervent prayer" of the righteous. We understand why the disciples, even after long months of observing the prayer life of Jesus, still asked him to teach them how to pray.

Mainline Protestantism is seeking to discover its identity and purpose. Careful observers are suggesting our uncertainty stems from a spiritual crisis. We do not know who we are nor what we are to do because we have lost touch with our devotional roots. Yearning for a better understanding of the miracle and mystery of prayer, we seek guidance outside the realm of

Christian experience. Today even some Christians seek to be informed about spirituality by turning to Eastern mysticism, occultism, and their secularized psychological counterparts. But no Christian need step beyond the boundaries of his or her own religious tradition in order to experience greater spiritual realities. This is the central affirmation of the author.

This book has the New Testament as its focus. Rather than giving major attention to the devotional classics or contemporary writings about the subject of prayer, the author has returned to original sources in scripture. Primary emphasis is upon the way in which the early church found power, authority, healing, and salvation in and through the name of Jesus.

The author suggests that we may on occasion pray just by breathing the holy name of Jesus itself, slowly and deliberately, quietly and reverently, over and again. This enables us to focus our attention upon the reality of God's presence and to be sensitive and responsive to the promptings of the Spirit. The name of Jesus is not to be used for magical purposes, nor as a way to control or influence God. It was a common name but was and is given authority because our prayers are in the name of Jesus, the Christ!

Shortly after our marriage, my wife's saintly mother would on occasion ride in the car with us. I was young and perhaps drove faster than was appropriate. If frightened, she would say softly, "Jesus, Jesus!" At first I thought this was quaint (though understandable because she was a godly person). As I grew older, I realized there are periods when a person is too distracted, weary, or ill to have the necessary attention span for carefully articulated prayers. Prayer, in its most effective form, may be the repetition, in childlike simplicity, of the name of Jesus.

Many will find the chapters "Sharing the Name with Others" and "Naming the Name for Others" most helpful. United Methodism was founded as an evangelistic movement. The vision of Francis Asbury was that the gospel should be preached in every kitchen. Many Christians feel uneasy about sharing their faith with others. The author encourages us to develop the skills, through practice, of sharing the name of Jesus with others and naming his name for others. In this way we combine evangelism and intercessory prayer. The effective strategy of the early church is suggested by a passage from scripture: "Day after day, in the temple courts and from house to house, they never stopped teaching and proclaiming the good news that Jesus is the Christ" (Acts 5:42).

I believe a careful study of this slender

volume could assist both the individual Christian and the church in a deepened life of prayer and authentic witness. At the heart of our endeavor is the realization that "where two or three come together in my name, there am I with them" (Matt. 18:20) and the greatest argument for the validity of Christianity is an exemplary life, lived in the power and presence of Jesus. "Whatever you do, whether in word or deed, do it all in the name of the Lord Jesus" (Col. 3:17).

Emerson S. Colaw
Bishop, Minnesota Area
United Methodist Church

Through Jesus, therefore, let us continually offer to God a sacrifice of praise—the fruit of lips that confess his name.

—Hebrews 13:15

Introduction

Ours is a society that confuses activity with progress and often mistakes frantic efforts to dissipate nervous energy for industriousness. We are made to feel guilty about doing nothing and, therefore, live our lives in perpetual motion. This type of thinking even influences the life of the church. The general impression is that if we are not doing something for the Lord, then we are not very committed as Christians. And "doing something" is usually thought of as some highly visible or publicly commendable activity.

We have the mistaken impression that Christianity essentially involves doing something when in reality it is trusting Someone to be with us and help us when we need help most. Multitudes of people who already belong to the church are spiritually undernourished and frustrated because they do not recognize and acknowledge their need to be with Jesus in a consciously meaningful way. For them Christianity has nothing more to offer than a ceaseless round of activities—classes to teach or attend, people on whom to call, committees on which to serve, bazaars, bake sales, and other work projects to support—so that the needs of various groups may be met.

Whenever we look at the program calendar of any church we soon discover that a strong church is assumed to be an active church in which there is always something going on. But in far too many instances the activities have become a substitute for spiritual vitality instead of a means of expressing that vitality. As a result, people who are active church members become depressed, discouraged, disillusioned, frustrated, and exhausted. They eventually conclude that if this is all that Christianity has to offer them, it is not enough to keep them interested. That which should enable them to stand up to life has become just another burden for them to carry, and they often drop out of church life completely.

In the midst of such spiritual exhaustion Jesus says to us, "Come to me, all you who are weary and burdened, and I will give you rest"

(Matt. 11:28). How desperately we need to learn to rest in Christ Jesus and be at peace with ourselves, with God, and with other people. We have a great need to touch Jesus and be touched by him in the depths of our being. But, practically speaking, we may not know where or how to begin. Our friends, including the clergy, may be unable to help us because they are being victimized by the same spiritual exhaustion that has us in its grip.

This spiritual need which lies deeply buried within us is experienced as an inner longing. What, if anything, can we do to make ourselves come alive spiritually? How can we regain our mental clarity, emotional stability, moral integrity, strength of will, physical stamina, and spiritual vitality? How do we enter into the Lord's rest and feed on Christ in our hearts by faith with thanksgiving?

Jesus described himself as the source of spiritual vitality for us even as a vine gives life to its branches. Far too many of us, however, are what Lloyd John Oglivie once described as "cut-flower Christians" who are pretty to look at for a time, but destined to wither and die. Yet, at the point of our need, Jesus comes to bring us an everlasting and irrepressible quality of life. We do not have to continue living as dying people in a dying world.

We need to be reconnected to our life-source in Jesus. We often sense that prayer has something to do with this reconnection process, but sometimes even our attempts to pray are faltering and ineffective. This could be because we tend to pray for the wrong reasons: to keep up appearances and out of a sense of duty. In that respect we are like the scribes and Pharisees who turned a genuinely helpful spiritual exercise into an effort in futility. We may go through the motions and rituals of prayer without ever having touched spiritual realities. Some people actually fall asleep without intending to while praying. If that is our problem, perhaps what we have to tell God isn't worth saying. Maybe we are wasting God's time as well as ours. We could be like the little girl who once told her mother concerning her bedtime prayers that she thought God was tired of hearing all that "now I lay me down to sleep stuff," so she told him the story of "Goldilocks and the Three Bears."

There is a certain superficiality about prayer which permeates some people's thinking and causes them to confuse saying or thinking many words with authentic prayer. However, it is not what we say but the spirit in which we say it that counts. We may want desperately to improve and deepen our prayer life. We may be having real struggles in prayer and trying ever so hard without getting any positive results. That is probably because we have yet to experience that grace-filled prayer which is the natural outgrowth of a life filled with a sense of God's presence.

Many of us sometimes secretly suspect that we have missed something in prayer. We want to grow and mature in this realm of Christian experience. That is why so many books on prayer continue to be published and read every year. That is why sermons about prayer get such a positive response. We want to learn more about the miracle and mystery of prayer. Unfortunately, much of the guidance that is available to us on this topic is outside the realm of Christian experience. It comes from Far Eastern mysticism, occultism, or one of their secularized psychological counterparts. But Christianity has more to offer us at this point than any other religion or philosophy. No Christian should feel the need to step beyond the boundaries of his or her own religious tradition in order to experience greater spiritual realities. Our mystical yearnings may be addressed in other teachings, but Christianity is far from devoid of these deeper mysteries and experiences.

In Luke's account of our Lord's visit with Martha and Mary (Luke 10:38–42) we find two contrasting responses to Jesus' presence. Martha is busy serving the Master and meeting his needs. Mary sits at his feet, enthralled by his teachings and so enamored with his presence that she is oblivious to everything else. Martha scolds Mary, or tries to get Jesus to scold her, for neglecting her duties as hostess. But Jesus tells Martha that she is all in a dither over nothing. Mary has chosen the role that is best for her at that particular moment. The implication is that if Martha were spiritually mature, then Mary's response to Jesus would not bother her. After all, Mary did not seem to be bothered by Martha's incessant activity. She made no attempt to scold Martha for doing her chores and fluttering about the kitchen instead of spending time with Jesus.

One of the marks of authentic spirituality is our tolerance of those whose beliefs and experience may differ from our own. When we are secure in our faith, then we do not have to continually defend ourselves or correct others. Life in Christ Jesus does not have to be an either-or proposition. It does not have to be an incessant round of meaningless activity, and it should not be filled with idle contemplation that is disassociated from the material world in which we live. We do not need more Marthas or more Marys in the church. We need more people whose lives express a healthy balance between prayer and other types of activity.

We do not have to join a monastery, go on a weekend retreat, or even set aside thirty minutes each day for uninterrupted meditation and contemplation in order to be with Jesus. We need not be in a church sanctuary on our knees, with our head bowed and our eyes closed, in order to pray effectively. Part of what it means for us to worship God "in spirit and truth" (John 4:23) is the joyous realization that we can pray anytime and anywhere. Paul admonished us to "pray without ceasing" (1 Thess. 5:17, KJV). Jesus said that we should always pray and not give up (Luke 18:1).

Such a life of unceasing prayer that would meet our spiritual needs while allowing us to continue other activities needs a focus and a strategy in order to prevent the noise and distractions of life from crowding it out. There are those who sense their own spiritual frustration and emptiness but experience a real struggle in prayer. In conversation with such people, I can sometimes discern a deep spiritual yearning in their lives.

Approaches to prayer differ with personal temperament, but one thing I have learned for certain as a pastor and spiritual counselor: If we are going to pursue an interior life of unceasing prayer and thereby experience continual spiritual nourishment, we need a prayer of centering that will enable us to get in touch with spiritual realities. We need something that we can carry in our hearts and minds throughout our day which represents the very essence of our faith.

For many people, the key to effectiveness in prayer lies in praying the name of Jesus repeatedly, continually, and authoritatively. Since Jesus is the source of our spiritual power and vitality, to have his name in our thoughts and prayers is to experience his strength and influence at work in our lives. Throughout the centuries Christians have found that praying the name of Jesus enabled them to experience the reality of Jesus. This practice has been greatly neglected by Christians in the Western world. Today, however, multitudes of spiritual adventurers are seeking to expand their awareness of deeper levels of spirituality and report that they have gained life-centering, mentally clarifying, and spiritually energizing results from praying the name of Jesus. I am not making reference to offering prayers in Jesus' name, but praying repeatedly and continually the name of Jesus as a point of focus and object of devotion in prayer.

Jesus is the door through which we can enter into deeper spiritual realities at our own individualized pace. It is up to us to pray the name of Jesus until we experience the person of Jesus and receive the vitality of Jesus into our lives in fresh new ways. Jesus is a friend on whom we can call anytime and anywhere—when we are lonely, depressed, discouraged, tired, worried, frightened, need help, or just want someone to listen. "Jesus Christ is the same yesterday and today and forever" (Heb. 13:18) for those who have learned to call on his name. His power and influence are still available to us today whenever we are willing to center our hearts and minds in him, receiving from him that which he wants to give us.

Would you like to deepen your prayer and devotional life? Are you struggling in your efforts to concentrate in prayer? Would you like to be able to pray without ceasing and live every moment of the day in fellowship with Jesus? Do not give up hope! There is something positive and life affirming that you can do to strengthen yourself spiritually. You have not exhausted every spiritual resource or explored every spiritual alternative if you have not tried praying the name of Jesus. You may experience new dimensions of spirituality that were previously unknown to you, as "everyone who calls on the name of the Lord will be saved" (Acts 2:21).

1. There Is Power in Jesus' Name

There is tremendous power and spiritual vitality in Jesus' name just waiting to be released when his followers begin to use his name in the way that he originally intended it to be used. Those early Christians were well aware of that fact. "Day after day, in the temple courts and from house to house, they never stopped teaching and proclaiming the good news that Jesus is the Christ" (Acts 5:42). They knew that it is not enough to refer to him as Savior, the Christ, or even Lord. No title alone is sufficient to express the reality of his presence. It is the name of Jesus that brings God's powerful presence into meaningful focus.

Sometimes we can learn as much from a

general overview of scripture as we can from specific texts. The general pattern found in the New Testament suggests to me that the activity of the Holy Spirit, the expression of spiritual gifts, and the church's evangelistic zeal and effectiveness tended to decline or increase with a corresponding decline or increase in the use of Jesus' name in prayers and conversation.

God's power was not weakened with the passing of time or dependent upon the people's enthusiasm and faith for its effectiveness. It was the name of Jesus that enabled the early Christians to release God's power in their own lives and the lives of others. Whenever they dared to use "the name that is above every name" (Phil. 2:9), God's kingdom always benefited.

It is hard to argue with results. Therefore, the religious leaders and authorities had the Apostles beaten and "ordered them not to speak in the name of Jesus" (Acts 5:40). But the Apostles rejoiced "because they had been counted worthy of suffering disgrace for the Name" (Acts 5:41). The Apostle Paul spoke of a day when "at the name of Jesus every knee should bow . . . and every tongue confess that Jesus Christ is Lord, to the glory of God the Father" (Phil. 2:10).

The power of God was active in the lives of those early Christians in ways that most Christians today seldom experience, because they had the advantage of functioning on a first-name basis with the Lord of the universe. Words like Christ, Master, and son of God are titles of *respect*. Other titles like Savior, Lord, and Redeemer describe what Jesus *does*. To call someone by his or her title is an expression of respect for that person. But to seek to relate to others on a first-name basis indicates a desire on our part to become more personally involved in their lives and have them become more intimately involved in our lives. The good news for us today is that we, too, can operate on a first-name basis with the Lord of the universe and thereby appropriate his strength and power— even as those first Christians so evidently did—because there is power in the name of Jesus.

Salvation Bestowing Power

Simon Peter told the Jewish religious leaders of his day concerning Jesus, "Salvation is found in no one else, for there is no other name under heaven given to men by which we must be saved" (Acts 4:12). Later he said to Cornelius in Caesarea, "All the prophets testify about him that everyone who believes in him receives forgiveness of sins through his name" (Acts

27

10:43). John's Gospel tells us that to believe in his name is to receive the right to become children of God—born of God's own Spirit (John 1:12–13). In Romans 10:13 and Acts 2:21 we are told that "everyone who calls on the name of the Lord will be saved." Those words are a direct quotation from the Old Testament found in Joel 2:32. The word *everyone* is an all-inclusive word. It means anyone—including you and me. Everyone who calls on the name of the Lord will be saved. And what is the Lord's name? The angel Gabriel said to Joseph in a dream concerning Mary's child, "You are to give him the name Jesus, because he will save his people from their sins" (Matt. 1:21).

One of the reasons more people today are not being saved (delivered from slavery to sin and the powers of darkness) is that they are not being taught to call upon the name of the Lord. Jesus is our only hope for salvation in this life as well as the next. We tend to think of the salvation that he offers us in terms of eternity instead of time. We see him as our ultimate savior but fail to experience him as our present source of help and the One who is always with us. We need to understand that salvation has a present tense as well as a past and future tense. It is not something relegated exclusively to yesterday or tomorrow. Today is the day of salvation. We can call on the name of the Lord and be saved today from whatever threatens to overwhelm us. He will either change our present circumstances or our attitude toward them, if we will surrender ourselves and our situation to him. This is the very structure of spiritual reality that we are affirming. If we trust Jesus completely, we will not be vulnerable to embarrassment or disappointment (Rom. 10:11).

Life-Changing Power

The reality of Jesus is at the very heart and center of the universe. T.S. Eliot was an agnostic but later became a Christian. He once wrote concerning Jesus, "He is the still point of the turning world." There is life-centering, physically-healing, spiritually-energizing power in the name of Jesus. Calling on his name strengthens our will, clarifies our thinking, and stabilizes our emotions. It never occurred to me that this is the case until I began to examine the lives of those for whom Jesus is a living presence and an active power and influence.

Calling on his name helps us to center our hearts and minds in his presence, thereby enabling us to touch Jesus and be touched by him in the center of our beings. This awakens us to the reality of his presence in that deeper part of our personalities. The more frequently we speak his name, the more fully he dwells in our hearts. Thus, our lives become integrated around the central reality of Jesus who is himself our source of life.

Calling on his name helps us to be more like Jesus. It cleanses our thoughts from sin and the influences of evil. We are enabled to dis-associate ourselves from defeatist attitudes and negative thinking. As we focus our attention upon Jesus we begin to understand that God is like Jesus and that God intends for us to be like Jesus—in power and glory, in attitude and outlook. We are changed into Jesus' likeness by beholding him and allowing our thoughts to be captivated by his thoughts.

The Power to Be Spiritually Fulfilled

Calling on Jesus' name is a cure for spiritual apathy because it allows his spirit and mind to awaken and energize our spirits and minds. As a result we become more energetic, enthusiastic, creative, innovative, and more fully committed to God's kingdom. The name of Jesus bestows his spiritual presence and power upon us which leads to our own personal spiritual fulfillment.

In response to Peter's sermon on the day of

Pentecost, the people asked him, "What shall we do?" Peter told them, "Repent and be baptized, every one of you, in the name of Jesus Christ so that your sins may be forgiven. And you will receive the gift of the Holy Spirit" (Acts 2:38). To repent means to let go of, leave behind, turn our backs on, or change our minds about something. It means that we receive and express a new attitude toward sin and salvation in our lives. To be baptized is to identify ourselves with Jesus Christ and his cause through involvement with a local fellowship of believers. The reference to forgiveness of sins means that we have received and accepted God's forgiveness so that we are fully cleansed from all unrighteousness. It is not something that we simply affirm in our minds. We also experience it in our hearts. Receiving the gift of the Holy Spirit means that our innermost self is spiritually awakened and fulfilled by that Spirit which comes from God.

The Holy Spirit comes to us in and through the name of Jesus. Our Lord himself said that "the Counselor, the Holy Spirit, whom the Father will send in my name, will teach you all things and will remind you of everything I have said to you" (John 14:26). If we want to be spiritually fulfilled, we will call upon the name of the Lord.

The Power to Heal

The glorified Jesus said of his future disciples that, among a number of spectacular things, "in my name they will . . . . place their hands on sick people, and they will get well" (Mark 16:17–18). Jesus possessed the ability to restore people to health and wholeness with a word or a touch. He shared that ability with his first disciples, and he continues to share that ability with his present-day disciples when they dare to minister unto others in his name.

Healing the sick was one of the primary ways that Jesus authenticated his earthly incarnational ministry. The continued healing of the sick in the life of the early church was the primary evidence that Jesus was authenticating his earthly spiritual ministry through the hands of those who touched the sick and prayed for their healing in his name. It is a ministry that has often been overlooked in the contemporary church, but Christians today are beginning to rediscover the healing power that is available to us in Jesus' name.

The Authority of His Name

When the seventy-two followers of Jesus returned from their preaching and healing mission, they reported to him, "Lord, even the demons submit to us in your name" (Luke 10:17). The name of Jesus carries with it the authority of Jesus to command and disperse evil powers, destructive forces, oppressive attitudes, and negative influences that seek to destroy us. By using Jesus' name we can exercise the power and authority to deliver ourselves and others from these destructive influences.

We have greatly neglected this aspect of prayer ministry in Jesus' name. Let us use the authority of his name with an open mind and heart for the meeting of our own needs and the needs of others. In the name of the One to whom all power and authority has been given in heaven and on earth (Matt. 28:18), we can do far more that we have dared to believe or ever suspected possible. Freedom from destructive tendencies and harmful habits can be ours. The oppressive spirits of extreme fear, guilt, despair, rage, grief, or depression can often be rebuked and dispersed in Jesus' name so that the spiritually afflicted person experiences immediate deliverance.

Potential for Asking and Receiving

Our Lord once told his disciples, "I will do whatever you ask in my name, so that the Son may bring glory to the Father. You may ask me for anything in my name, and I will do it" (John 14:13–14). To ask in Jesus' name is to be assured of an answer that will glorify the heavenly Father. That does not mean that God is reluctant to help us unless or until we can somehow get Jesus to plead our case for us. God is more eager to help us than we are to receive God's help. Asking in Jesus' name gives us the confidence to ask for help, assured that God will indeed meet all our needs from the glorious riches in Christ Jesus (Phil. 4:19).

Yes, there is power in Jesus' name! And we have neglected to avail ourselves of it because we have failed to understand that spiritual power is expressed in direct relation to our praying the name of Jesus. Once we have learned to effectively use the name that is above every name, renewed spiritual power and vitality will be ours.

Action Response

1. Try saying repeatedly to yourself, "Jesus Christ is Lord." Say it slowly and deliberately, emphasizing a different word each time.

   > *Jesus* Christ is Lord.
   > Jesus *Christ* is Lord.
   > Jesus Christ *is* Lord.
   > Jesus Christ is *Lord.*

   You may want to use this affirmation several times daily for a week or more just to see what happens.

2. Think about the implications of what you have affirmed. When is Jesus Christ Lord of your life? Is he only your Lord when things run smoothly, or is he also your Lord when you find yourself in some valley of frustration and despair?

3. When and under what circumstances did you first consciously embrace Jesus Christ as your Savior and Lord? What were the results?

2. The Prayer of the Heart

Most people think of prayer as an audible activity which calls for the cessation of all other activities. There can also be an inwardness of prayer which does not interfere with other activities and produces no outward, visible indications that it is taking place. There can be a continual prayer of the heart and mind which does not interrupt our daily routine. There can be such a profound prayerfulness at the center of our beings that our entire lives are saturated with prayer. We need to rediscover the inwardness of prayer and the miraculous potential for having a continual inner communion with our Lord.

Prayer is a very personal and private

matter in which we must find our own way with the Lord's help. He has in mind for each of us a way of prayer that is suited to our specific needs and temperament. What I am going to suggest in the next few pages is a way of praying that may be unfamiliar to you. I invite you to consider it with an open mind and an open heart as a possible option for your own prayer life. I encourage you to be a spiritual adventurer. You may be delighted with the results.

A Deeper Way of Praying

There is a way of praying that goes deeper and requires more of us than most of our efforts at prayer. It is the prayer of the innermost self, the prayer of the heart that never stops resonating to the vibrations of Jesus' own spirit of prayer. The mind can sometimes cooperate with the spirit in prayer. At other times the conscious mind is preoccupied with outward duties and responsibilities. The prayer of the heart is a way of bypassing our conscious thought processes and preoccupations so that we can pray from within the deeper levels of our personality. It is not altogether the result of conscious effort or strength of will. Rather, it arises from the inner spiritual promptings that we experience with varying degrees of intensity. It is in a very real sense the outpouring of our spiritual energy flow.

The prayer of the innermost self begins with contemplation and results in an ongoing sense of abiding in God's presence. It eventually becomes almost second nature to us, so that our entire day and even the night is filled with prayer. The prayer takes on a life of its own and seems to pray itself. We may actually find ourselves praying as we fall asleep, wake up during the night still praying, and arise the next morning with a heart overflowing with prayer. Perhaps we were even praying at some unconscious level while we slept.

This inner life of continual prayer was most assuredly what Paul was referring to when he admonished his fellow Christians to "pray without ceasing" (1 Thess. 5:17, KJV). Such prayer may begin as the result of conscious effort or it may arise from within, prompted by God's own spirit. But either way the result is a prayer-filled life. It is a divinely originated, mystical experience and not something one earns by strenuous effort or spotless virtue. There is, however, something that we can do to prepare ourselves for a life of ceaseless prayer. We can center our thoughts in the reality of Jesus and be open to the possibilities of prayer without ceasing. That will make us ready to receive and express the prayer of the heart or the "Prayer of Jesus" as some choose to call it.

Dare we to believe that it is possible to practice the presence of Jesus and live in continual spiritual communion and conscious contact with him all of the time—wherever we go and whatever we may be doing? Yes, it is possible for us to live consciously in Jesus' presence for hours, days, and even weeks. The potential exists for us to live every hour of every day for the rest of our lives as well as all eternity with him. Throughout the centuries Christians have testified to the reality of this glorious possibility. Yes, what doubters have scoffed at and mystics have searched for we can receive and experience.

This potential for ceaseless prayer centered in Jesus has gone virtually unexplored in many contemporary Christian circles. Inner prayer should not be allowed to take the place of vocalized prayers or having a definite time apart with Christ during the day. In fact, it will enhance the power and effectiveness of other forms and times of prayer.

Getting Started

How does one begin to pray in a manner that transcends conscious words and thoughts?

Have you ever held a diamond under a light turning it first one way and then another in order to appreciate its multifaceted radiance? It is the same with contemplative prayer. In our consciousness we can use the name of Jesus as the object of devotion and the focus of our contemplation. By doing this we can center our attention in the reality of Jesus and consider our relatedness to him from different points of view. Praying the name of Jesus in this manner enables us to repeatedly return to him in our thoughts and thereby build our thought-life and actions around him. The goal of this procedure is to enable us to live continually in the presence and in the strength of our Lord.

One Pilgrim's Way

There is a form of contemplative prayer which has been used for centuries in the Eastern Orthodox Church that is unfamiliar to most of us in the Western Church. This form of prayer and its results are recorded in a book called *The Way of a Pilgrim*, which tells the story of one Christian pilgrim's travels in Russia and Siberia. The book also gives details concerning how this unknown pilgrim learned and sometimes taught others *a special way of praying*.

The pilgrim begins his spiritual quest in

response to scripture by asking himself and others the question of how one goes about fulfilling the scriptural admonition to "pray without ceasing." The answer to that question and its consequences compose the bulk of the text.

Very early in the story the pilgrim meets a monk in a monstery who helps him understand the true meaning of unceasing prayer. The monk suggests to him as a prayer focus the form of prayer known as the "Jesus Prayer" or the "Prayer of Jesus"—"Lord Jesus Christ, have mercy on me." In other literature this same prayer takes on various forms and adaptations, such as: "Lord Jesus Christ, Son of God, have mercy upon me, a sinner." One of its simplest forms is to breathe the holy name of Jesus itself, slowly and deliberately, saying quietly and reverently, "Jesus, Jesus, Jesus."

Here is what the monk tells the pilgrim concerning the prayer of the heart or prayer without ceasing:

> The continuous interior Prayer of Jesus is a constant uninterrupted calling upon the divine Name of Jesus with the lips, in the spirit, in the heart; while forming a mental picture of His constant presence, and imploring His grace, during every occupation, at all times, in all

places, even during sleep. The appeal is couched in these terms, "Lord Jesus Christ, have mercy on me." One who accustoms himself to this appeal experiences as a result so deep a consolation and so great a need to offer the prayer always, that he can no longer live without it, and it will continue to voice itself within him of its own accord. Now do you understand what prayer without ceasing is?

In the days that follow, the pilgrim is given detailed instructions concerning how to pray the name of Jesus repeatedly and continually until it becomes second nature to him—a spiritual habit. The whole idea is that one prays the prayer repeatedly until the prayer begins to pray itself or until it is being prayed silently, inwardly, and continually with hardly any conscious effort at all.

In one instance the monk tells him, "Whether you are standing or sitting, walking or lying down, continually repeat 'Lord Jesus Christ, have mercy on me.'" He then admonishes the pilgrim to "say it quietly and without fail exactly three thousand times a day without deliberately increasing or diminishing the number. God will help you and by this means you will reach also the unceasing activity of the heart."

Later, the pilgrim tells of the results of his praying in this special way and how it has enabled him to strengthen his prayer and devotional life. He feels that the "Prayer of Jesus" has ceased coming from his lips and begun praying itself in his heart or spirit. What once was mental prayer has become for him spiritual prayer that goes deeper than conscious thought processes and mental imagery. The "Prayer of Jesus" is for him a form of prayer that leads to a life of prayer. Eventually the form ceases but the prayer continues. Let the pilgrim himself describe to you the results of his experiments with the "Jesus Prayer":

> That is how I go about now, and ceaselessly repeat the Prayer of Jesus, which is more precious and sweet to me than anything in the world. At times I do as much as forty-three or four miles a day, and do not feel that I am walking at all. I am aware only of the fact that I am saying my Prayer. When the bitter cold pierces me, I begin to say my Prayer more earnestly and I quickly get warm all over. When hunger begins to overcome me, I call more often on the Name of Jesus, and I forget my wish for food. When I fall ill and get rheumatism in my back and legs, I fix my thoughts on the Prayer and do not notice the pain. If

anyone harms me I have only to think,
"How sweet is the Prayer of Jesus!" and
the injury and anger alike pass away and
I forget it all.

Apparently, he has found a way of prayer that is very meaningful to him and meets his deepest spiritual needs.

Finding Our Own Way

Like that anonymous pilgrim, it is up to each of us to discover our own way to pray from the heart continually. Such prayer would involve the totality of our beings: body, mind, and spirit. It would require a unique combination of self-effort and self-surrender and the sensitivity to know which is needed at any given moment. Such a spirit of prayer has the potential for saturating our beings to the extent that our entire life become a prayer. As I suggested previously, even when the conscious mind sleeps, the heart or spirit may continue to pulsate with prayer. We have within us the potential for making such prayer a habit until it becomes an instinct which makes it a ceaseless activity.

Some may object to such repetitious forms of prayer on the grounds that Jesus once said that we should not "keep on babbling like pagans, for they think that they will be heard because of their many words" (Matt. 6:7). But those who offer objections on such grounds have misunderstood what our Lord was saying and what we are trying to accomplish through praying the name of Jesus in this special way. The whole point of Jesus' remark was to counteract a pagan misconception about God which teaches that one can wear down God's resistance and thereby change God's mind concerning something if one persists in pleading one's case. We do not change God's will or mind by our pleading. And we do not gain an audience with the Lord of the universe through the use of eloquent words. The objective of authentic prayer is not to align God's will with ours, but to align our will with God's. Praying the name of Jesus does not change God's attitude toward us in any way. It enables us to focus our attention upon the reality of God's presence and to be more sensitive and responsive to the promptings of the Holy Spirit.

The "Jesus Prayer" is one man's approach to praying continually from his innermost self. One is instructed to pray the prayer of the mind or intentional will until it becomes the prayer of the heart and spirit. It is then almost an effortless form of prayer continually offered from the depths of our being. This may not be the way of praying that the Lord has chosen for you, but let me urge you to explore in some form the potential of inner prayer that is centered in the name of Jesus. Once we have been sensitized to the inner vibrations of the spirit of God within us, we will find a peace and joy that will enable us to triumph in any situation.

In the final analysis, the authentic "Prayer of Jesus" is the prayer that Jesus himself offers in and through us by the power of his Holy Spirit. As we surrender our prayer and devotional lives to him, he uses our spirits, hearts, and minds as channels through which to express his desires and concerns for us and others.

In teaching us to pray, Jesus gives each of us a prayer vocabulary that is uniquely our own. I am not referring to glossolalia or "praying in tongues," although some may consider that to be their prayer language. I am talking about the language of the spirit which meets our deepest needs, expresses our innermost concerns, and goes beyond that to express our Lord's needs and concerns.

Prayer is something more than that which we do with our minds. It also involves our hearts and spirits—that deeper part of our personalities to which only the Spirit of Jesus has access. Prayer in its highest form requires more than conscious effort. It also requires the

47

surrender of our innermost selves to Jesus, giving him permission to make our lives a continually flowing fountain of unceasing prayer. When we have learned how to do that, we will have discovered the secret of the prayer of the heart.

Action Response

1. As often as you think of it today, make a conscious effort to pray the "Jesus Prayer" as it is printed here:

    > Lord Jesus Christ,
    > Son of God,
    > Have mercy upon me,
    >   a sinner.

2. Does this approach to prayer appeal to you? Why or why not?

3. Was it difficult for you to pray this prayer silently, repeatedly, and continually? Why or why not?

4. In what way was this prayer experience helpful? What did it teach you about yourself and the Lord?

3. The Reality Behind the Name

One of the greatest needs that we have in our spiritual lives is to learn how to properly use the power and authority of Jesus' name. We can only do that by getting in touch with the reality behind the name. Prayer is more than just mouthing words. It is experiencing and expressing spiritual realities in such a way that either we ourselves are changed or our situation is changed in some positive manner. To "keep on babbling like pagans" (Matt. 6:7), a practice which our Lord condemned, means that we continue to express meaningless words in our prayers which hold little if any inner relevance. It indicates that we are praying off the top of our heads instead of from the bottom of our hearts.

There are those for whom the name of our sovereign Lord is simply an expletive. Others use his name by closing their prayers with the words "in Jesus' name" without knowing what it really means to pray in his name. Our Lord's name should never be used in an irreverent or superficial manner.

In order to pray the name of Jesus effectively, it must well up from within the innermost self as an expression of deeper spiritual realities. It is a privilege to be able to call on his name and thereby enter into his presence and experience deliverance in our hour of need. But privilege also brings with it the responsibility of using wisely that which has been given to us. This means that we do not casually rattle off the name of our Lord without giving thought to the reality which his name expresses. Some people recite the Lord's Prayer or the Twenty-third Psalm in such a thoughtless manner, but that is not the essence of authentic prayer.

When we tack the phrase "in Jesus' name" onto the end of our prayers, this does not mean that we can give God orders. We do not write our own ticket with God by asking in Jesus' name. Instead, we allow God to write the ticket. Then we accept it and let God send us wherever he wants us to go. To pray in Jesus' name means that we allow our wills to be aligned with the heavenly Father's will so that we express the spirit of the son of God in our prayers.

The Danger of Abusing the Name

It would be highly unwise to attempt to use Jesus' name for magical purposes, as a good luck charm, or as a way to control or influence God. Such abuse of the name of God's son can have disastrous results as the seven sons of Sceva discovered. They had witnessed the power and authority expressed through Jesus' name by his followers, but they had failed to make a personal connection between the name of Jesus and the reality behind the name. They tried to exorcise an evil spirit from a man by commanding it to leave the man alone "in the name of Jesus whom Paul preaches" (Acts 19:13). But the evil spirit cried out through the man it had possessed, "I know Jesus and I know Paul, but who are you to be giving me orders?" (Acts 19:15, AP) Then the spiritually afflicted man attacked them with demonic fury and gave all seven of them a severe beating. If we would presume to use the name of Jesus effectively we must get in touch with the reality behind the name, so that our hearts will be in tune with God and the power of Jesus' name will not be abused or compromised.

What's in a Name

There is no inherent magic in the name of Jesus. But his name does represent to us a spiritual reality and a historic personality. Shakespeare suggested that a rose by any other name smells just as sweet. It is not the name that counts but the reality which the name represents and the personal associations that we have with that reality. If we lived in a world where roses were called *onions*, we would be sending our sweethearts bouquets of onions without apology.

Actually, Jesus was a name that was quite common in biblical times. In the New Testament we find several men with some form of the word *Jesus* in their name. Elymas was a sorcerer and a false prophet who was also called Bar-Jesus or "Son of Jesus" (Acts 13:6–11). There were Judas Iscariot who betrayed our Lord with a kiss and Judas Thaddaeus, another one of our Lord's disciples, whose names were related to the name of Jesus in a manner similar to that which Will, Bill, and William are related. Joshua, from the Old Testament, is another name closely linked to the name of Jesus.

The whole point is that had our Lord's name been Thomas or Samuel it would have been just as effective because his name expresses his power and reality. In the words of a well-known hymn, "Jesus, the very thought of thee with sweetness fills the breast." Whenever we call upon the name of Jesus we are referring to a certain man who lived at a particular time in history and in a specific location. We are talking about Jesus of Nazareth, the carpenter's son, Mary's child—also known as the Christ and the son of the living God. Jesus is his name and the Christ, or God's Anointed One, is his title.

To receive Jesus into our lives is to trust in his name and begin to express our potential for being true children of God (John 1:12). To experience the reality which that name represents will result in our having his name foremost in our thoughts. "They will see his face, and his name will be on their foreheads" (Rev. 22:4). We only begin to use our Lord's name effectively in prayer when we seek through his name a personal experience of the reality of Jesus.

Who Jesus Is

The astonishing claim of the early church that literally turned their society upside down was the affirmation that Jesus is the Christ. Jesus of Nazareth is God's long-expected messiah, the Lord of the universe and the author of life. To say that Christ is Lord is not a very spectacular claim. It would not take much faith to say that God's Anointed One is Lord. But when we affirm that *Jesus* is Lord, that is quite a different matter. Here is a specific man, who lived and breathed and taught and ministered among us. And what we are saying is that God is like Jesus and we are destined to be like Jesus in attitude and outlook—in power and glory!

The reality of Jesus is both an objective reality and a subjective experience. Because of his historic context and identification with humankind in a certain day and age, we can say certain things about his nature and personality. The reality of Jesus has been and continues to be expressed in different ways through different cultures and through a variety of personalities. Nevertheless, he is clearly recognizable because of the consistency of his continuing revelation with his initial revelation during New Testament times.

Our Lord once asked his disciples, "Who do you say that I am?" Simon Peter, speaking for the rest of the group, responded, "You are the Christ, the Son of the Living God" (Matt. 16:16). And Jesus told him that the personal recognition and acknowledgement of who he (Jesus) is would be a foundation upon which he would build his church. "What must we do to do the work of God?" some people asked him on another occasion. Jesus replied, "The work of God is this: to believe in the one he has sent" (John 6:29).

A young minister had trouble being accepted as a candidate for ordination in his denomination because, in spite of the fact that he affirmed that Christ and God are one, he could not affirm that Jesus is God. It is indeed easier to say that Christ is Lord than to say that Jesus is Lord. In fact, the Apostle Paul wrote that nobody can truly say that Jesus is Lord without the enabling power of the Holy Spirit (1 Cor. 12:3, AP). Such recognition and affirmation of the lordship of Jesus is the authentic expression of a personal spiritual awakening.

The Power of the Reality

The person who uses the power and authority of Jesus' name effectively is in touch with the reality behind the name. Concerning a disciple of Jesus who was not of their official circle, our Lord once said, "No one who does a miracle in my name can in the next moment say anything bad about me" (Mark 9:39). The power of Jesus' name lies in the reality which his name represents. When Moses asked God what to tell Pharaoh and his associates should they ask who had sent him with the message of deliverance for the Israelites, he was told, "Tell them that *I Am*

57

sent you" (Exod. 3:14, AP). The Hebrew words for "I am" literally mean "I was who I was, I am who I am, I will be who I will be." The tense of the verb employed is unknown. But what it means is that in the past, present, and future, God is the self-determining One. Jesus made reference to this when he said to the Jews in the temple courtyard, "I told you that you would die in your sins; if you do not believe that I am the One I claim to be" (John 8:24). In reference to his death upon the cross he said, "When you have lifted up the Son of Man, then you will know who I am" (John 8:28). The statement that angered the religious leaders of his day most of all was when Jesus referred to his eternal existence as the divine son of God by saying "Before Abraham was born, I am!" (John 8:58). In Gethsemane when Judas Iscariot and the angry mob came with a detachment of soldiers and some religious leaders seeking to arrest Jesus of Nazareth, he confronted them saying, "I am he" (John 18:5). And John records in his Gospel that as an almost involuntary reflex the crowd drew back and fell to the ground (John 18:6). That enraged mob, the detachment of soldiers, and the religious leaders could not stand up against the power of the reality of Jesus. In fact, the only reason that they were able to take him was because he allowed them to take him (John

10:17–18). John's Gospel comes to a climax when Thomas sees the resurrected Jesus and exclaims, "My Lord and my God!" (John 20:28). Paul pointed to a day when "at the name of Jesus every knee should bow, in heaven and on earth and under the earth, and every tongue confess that Jesus Christ is Lord, to the glory of God the Father" (Phil. 2:9–11). Whether by personal acknowledgment or involuntary reflex there shall come a time when, as Isaac Watts writes, "Jesus shall reign where'er the sun does his successive journeys run." The glorious name of our wonderful Lord and the power and authority behind his name will eventually overcome all opposing forces.

A Soldier Acknowledges the Authority

A certain Roman centurion who had a critically ill servant came to Jesus seeking his help. It must have been a strange sight to those who witnessed it. Centurions were the strength of the Roman army. There were six thousand soldiers in a legion and these legions were divided up into units of one hundred fighting men. These units were called centuries. And the centurions were the commanding officers of these divisions of soldiers. They were the professional soldiers and officers who had proven

59

themselves in battle. They were brave and strong and possessed a sense of fair play. They were totally loyal to Caesar and had laid their lives on the line for him. As William Barclay notes in *The Gospel of Matthew* (vol. 1), "Every centurion mentioned in the New Testament is spoken of with honor and respect."

But this particular centurion had two characteristics that distinguished him from the rest. First, he cared for his servant as a person and wanted to do everything possible to help him get well. In a day and age when slaves were treated like possessions to be discarded when they were no longer useful, he was loyal to his servant and felt a responsibility toward him. Second, he recognized in Jesus a power and authority that most people only half suspected. He was a Gentile and Jesus was a Jew. The centurion knew that according to Jewish law and custom a Jew could not enter the home of a Gentile because it was considered to be ceremonially unclean. He did not, however, allow contemporary customs to prevent him from coming to Jesus and seeking his help.

So this centurion, who had sworn an oath of loyalty unto death to Caesar, walked briskly into Jesus' presence as the crowd parted to make way for him. He probably removed his helmet, placed it under his right arm, gestured with his left arm as he bowed and greeted Jesus with these words, "Lord, my servant lies at home paralyzed and in terrible suffering" (Matt. 8:6). A hush came over the crowd. Up until that time the centurion had never addressed anyone but Caesar as lord; therefore, his words must have stunned them into silence.

Jesus then said to the soldier, "You're acquainted with our customs, shall I go home with you and heal your servant?" But the centurion replied, "Look, I've thought about this situation and your being in my home really isn't necessary. I wouldn't want you to break your own religious traditions in order to help me. But I am a man in a position of authority. And I recognize authority when I see it. Therefore, just say the word and my servant will get well" (Matt. 8:7–9, AP).

In response to the soldier's recognition of his authority, Jesus remarked that he had not found anyone in all of Israel with such great faith (Matt. 8:10). Praise God for the eyes of faith to see who Jesus is and what he can do! Our Lord then told the man, "Go! It will be done just as you believed it would" (Matt. 8:13). And his servant was healed that very hour.

Would you also like to get in touch with the reality behind the name of Jesus? Read the four Gospels of Matthew, Mark, Luke, and John until you understand the kind of person Jesus was and continues to be. Seek to learn everything that you can about the life he lived, the attitudes he expressed, the teachings he shared, and the power and authority he displayed. Find out where he went and who he saw and how people responded to him. Learn how and why he died and also arose from the dead. Then, turn to Hebrews 13:8 where it says that Jesus Christ is the same yesterday, today, and forever. Begin to affirm the fact that who Jesus once was he still is, what Jesus once said and did he is still saying and doing. His power and authority have not been diminished by the passing of time. It is our failure to call on his name and experience his deliverance that has diminshed his power. And from now on when you read scripture, ask yourself, "What does this tell me about Jesus?"

Think about John's Gospel in which Jesus said, "I, when I am lifted up from the earth, will draw all men to myself" (John 12:32). In an immediate sense he was talking about his crucifixion. But in another sense, to lift up the name of Jesus is to be more closely drawn to the reality of Jesus. In Acts 2:21 we are told that everyone who calls on the name of the Lord will be saved. Start calling on his name today, and you will experience the joy of his salvation.

We can learn to rely on the power and

authority of the reality of Jesus in our lives and find our security, protection, and help in him. We can fight from a position of strength and victory in Jesus' name. Like the centurion, we can come to Jesus in our need and seek his help for ourselves and others. It does not matter what others may think. All that matters is that when we need help Jesus can give it. The victory that overcomes the world is our faith—not in ourselves, but in Jesus.

Action Response

1. As often as you think of it, try saying yes to the reality of Jesus in your life today. You may wish to use this prayer as a model:

   Yes, Jesus . . . Yes, Jesus . . . Yes, Jesus
   Yes, Jesus
   Yes, Jesus . . . Yes, Jesus . . . Yes, Jesus
   I say yes to you with all of my heart.

2. Have you truly said yes to Jesus and allowed him to take full charge of your life? What part of your life do you have the most difficulty letting Jesus control? Explain.

4. Sharing the Name with Others

Wilson O. Weldon, former World Editor of *The Upper Room,* once observed, "There is a reluctance on the part of modern Christians to name the name of Jesus in the pulpit and in daily conversation." In that one remark he went right to the heart of our present spiritual dilemma in the church. We tend to lose what we fail to share. If we want to keep Jesus in our thoughts and alive in our experience, we must tell others about him.

John's Gospel adds this editorial comment to Jesus' words about sending the Holy Spirit into our lives as streams of living water, "By this he meant the Spirit, whom those who believed in him were later to receive. Up to that time the

Spirit had not been given, since Jesus had not yet been glorified" (John 7:39). When this Gospel refers to the glorification of Jesus, it is concerned with a specific act in history, namely his crucifixion upon the cross for our redemption.

But seeking to apply this principle in a more general sense, we can say that when Jesus is glorified in our speech and actions, then the Spirit is given and received in fresh new ways. I wonder what would happen in our lives and the lives of those with whom we associate, if we would begin to call on his name more often—more spontaneously and unashamedly? What wondrous things could be accomplished? What miracles could be performed in Jesus' name?

Positive Confession Has Eternal Consequences

One of John's letters tells us, "Every spirit that acknowledges that Jesus Christ has come in the flesh is from God" (1 John 4:2). The Christian faith begins with a positive confession of faith in Jesus that leads to an experience of spiritual fulfillment in our innermost selves. The Apostle Paul once wrote. "That if you confess with your mouth, 'Jesus is Lord,' and believe in your heart that God raised him from the dead, you will be saved" (Rom. 10:9). One indication of spiritual maturity is the ability to use the name of Jesus with power, authority, conviction, and authenticity. It is only when Jesus has become real to us that we are able to make him real to others. This is one reason why so many Christians are reluctant to become involved in personal witnessing.

Taking advantage of every opportunity that comes our way to say a good word for Jesus strengthens our identification with him and his indentification with us. This has implications for both time and eternity. Jesus himself warned us, "Whoever acknowledges me before men, I will also acknowledge him before my Father in heaven. But whoever disowns me before men, I will disown him before my Father in heaven" (Matt. 10:32–33). We do not earn our own salvation through acknowledging Jesus as our Lord, but we could lose our only hope of salvation by our failure to acknowledge him.

This is not simply a profession of faith that our Lord is seeking from us but a confession of faith. It is not something that we profess to believe but Someone whom we claim to know— especially when it is costly to claim knowledge of him—that is being called for in this instance. It is not loyalty to a standard of conduct or a system of thought but loyalty to a person that determines our eternal destiny.

Roman citizens and residents of occupied territories were required to pay tribute to Caesar annually and thus affirm their loyalty to Rome. They were expected to pay taxes, burn some incense in a pagan temple, and affirm publicly that Caesar was lord. After they met these requirements, they were free to go out and worship as they pleased. But many radically dedicated Christians refused to make such a public statement, because they knew that only Jesus is Lord. Their refusal to acknowledge Caesar in the prescribed manner made them an enemy to the Roman government. As a result, they were imprisoned, tortured and often martyred.

However, it has been suggested that some ingenious Christians thought they had found a way to avoid such a fate. They thought they could burn incense in the temple and *pretend* to confess Caesar as lord without doing any harm since they *knew* that Jesus is truly Lord. It was to these people that the Apostle Paul was writing when he said that no one can say that Jesus is Lord without the enabling power of the Holy Spirit (1 Cor. 12:3). He was in effect saying to them, "Are you trusting in Jesus or in your own ingenuity for survival?" To say that Jesus is Lord when it is costly to do so requires the enabling power of the Holy Spirit. We cannot confess Jesus before others under adverse or hostile conditions in our own strength.

I belong to Jesus, and I am trusting him to help me cope with life's challenges. To whom or to what do you belong? We belong to that which we think about and talk about continually. We belong to that which we dwell upon. Whatever has your thoughts has you!

Seize the Opportunity

We are at our best whenever we are telling people about Jesus: what he has done for us and can do for them. Therefore, let us seize every opportunity to say a good word for Jesus. Learn to be a name dropper. Try casually and naturally naming the name that is above all names in conversation with others. I don't mean that we should talk about him all the time, but when the opportunity arises within the natural flow of conversation and subject matter, let us not hesitate to tell others about Jesus.

We do not need to give people our sympathy and understanding half as much as we need to give them our Jesus who was in all ways tempted as we are and yet did not allow himself to be separated from God the Father. People need to know that we care, but our concern is not enough unless we can also communicate to them the reality of Jesus. Whenever we refer others to Jesus, that is witnessing. When we refer Jesus to others, that is praying. We need to do both.

Every situation that we face in life—whether good or bad—is an opportunity to lift up the name of Jesus. When the reality of Jesus becomes greater than our problems, frustrations, sins, failures, shortcomings, hurts, anger, pain, and disease, then we experience his victory. To lift up the name of Jesus, affirm his victory over sin and death, and to acknowledge his continuing presence with those who trust him, means that we will always have a positive word of encouragement to offer others regardless of the situation or circumstances.

Have you ever wondered why the early church spread like wildfire? What was the secret of the phenomenal growth and evangelical effectiveness of those first Christians? Their secret strategy is given to us in the book of Acts where it is recorded, "Day after day, in the temple courts and from house to house, they never stopped teaching and proclaiming the good news that Jesus is the Christ" (Acts 5:42). They filled Jerusalem with their doctrines and turned the world upside down with their teachings about Jesus. That was the key to their success in evangelism. It is also the reason why, in spite of all of our programming and planning, we still are not growing numerically in the mainline Protestant congregations throughout our nation today.

We talk about evangelistic strategy and church growth but fail to mention the name of Jesus. Yet, it is obvious to anyone reading the book of Acts with an open heart and mind that the method of evangelization employed by the early church consisted primarily of lifting up the name of Jesus and trusting him to draw others to himself. Today we employ publicity campaigns and program strategies to promote our crusades, revivals, and missions. I think the early Christians would tell us that it is not our task to motivate people to come to Jesus. It is our responsibility to lift him up and trust him for the rest.

The Lord God has created every person with a desire to hear more about Jesus. The more they hear, the more they want to hear. Every person who belongs to Jesus wants to learn more about him and his will for our lives. When he is left out of a sermon, lesson, or book, it leaves people spiritually unfulfilled and hungry for the bread of heaven. But when we tell others about Jesus they keep coming back for more. We will be able to draw and keep more new people in the church by building up their faith and confidence in Jesus as Lord. We will be able to hold the attention of children, youth, and

71

adults because we are at our best when we are telling others about him. He is the greatest person who ever lived and the best friend we could ever have. The simplest way that we can introduce others to him is usually the most effective. Though non-Christians may seem skeptical at first, often they, too, want to learn more about Jesus. Perhaps they have seen some of the superficial values and traditions that have invaded the church. They may not speak the doctrinal language which we use in Christian circles. But somehow they sense that there is something about Jesus which demands investigation.

Preaching, teaching, writing, and counseling are most exciting and fulfilling to me, because they give me the opportunity to tell others about Jesus. Lifting up his name for others and seeing him meet their needs makes him more real to me also. Keeping Jesus in my thoughts helps me to keep him in my life. Keeping Jesus in my conversation helps me to keep him in my thoughts.

Howard Allred is one of the most effective pastor-evangelists that I have ever known. It took me years to understand that the reason for his effectiveness lies in the fact that he is always talking about Jesus. His conversation suggests that they are the best of friends, because his knowledge of Jesus arises out of a close personal association and not just theoretical speculation. Truly, he has learned the secret of sharing the name of the Lord with others.

To the early Christians the reality of Jesus was at the center of life. When talking with Jews they could refer to even the most obscure Old Testament passages of scripture and see Jesus in them. They were not always very systematic or consistent in their scriptural interpretations, but they managed to make their point. The Bible tells us that the secret of Philip's evangelistic power lay in the fact that the people "believed Philip as he preached the good news of the Kingdom of God and the name of Jesus" (Acts 8:12). Philip had a very successful ministry in a certain city in Samaria, but the Spirit prompted him to move out into a rural area. On a country road he encountered a chariot with an Ethiopian eunuch, an important official of the queen of Ethiopia, as its only passenger. As Philip ran along beside the chariot he heard the man reading scripture aloud as was the custom in those days. Philip noticed that he was reading from the prophet Isaiah. "Do you understand what you are reading?" Philip asked the eunuch. "How can I, unless someone instructs me?" the man replied. Then, sensing that Philip had knowledge of scripture, the man invited him to sit in his chariot while he read:

> He was led like a sheep to the slaughter,
>   and as a lamb before the shearer
>   is silent,
>   so he did not open his mouth.
> In his humiliation he was deprived
>   of justice.
>   Who can speak of his descendants?
>   For his life was taken from the earth.
>   —Acts 8:32–33; see Isaiah 53:7–8

The eunuch stopped reading and asked, "Who is the prophet describing? Is he referring to himself or someone else?" Philip saw his opportunity to share the gospel and immediately seized it, saying to the man, "Let me tell you about Jesus of Nazareth" (Acts 8:26–35, AP).

Those early Christians also believed that even without the rich religious heritage of the Jews, the Gentiles could still experience fullness of life in Jesus: "In his name shall the Gentiles trust" (Matt. 12:21, KJV). When Paul went to Athens their idols must have been offensive to his Jewish background which strictly forbade idol worship. But Paul did not condemn them for their paganism. Instead, he commended them for their religiosity. He said in effect, "I can see that you are a very religious people. You have many idols and pay tribute to many gods. In fact you even have one idol designated in tribute to an unknown god. Let me tell you about him and how you can get to know him" (Acts 17:22–31, AP).

When Simon Peter shared the name of Jesus with a paralytic by the temple gate, he was giving this man his most valuable posession. He said to the lame beggar, "Silver or gold I do not have, but what I have I give you. In the name of Jesus Christ of Nazareth, walk" (Acts 3:6). Then, he helped the man to his feet and he was healed instantly. The man who had formerly been unable to walk took one timid step and then another. He walked a little faster and tried jumping and leaping. He was even seen in the temple courts walking and leaping and praising God for his healing. Naturally, those who knew the man wanted to know what had happened to him that enabled him to be physically healed. Peter offered this explanation: "It is Jesus' name and the faith that comes through him that has given this complete healing to him, as you can all see" (Acts 3:16). So, Peter and John boldly and effectively shared the name of Jesus with Jew and Gentile alike even when the Jewish leaders "commanded them not to speak or teach at all in the name of Jesus" (Acts 4:18).

A Living Witness

The greatest argument for the validity of Christianity is an exemplary life that is lived in the power and presence of Jesus. This does not mean that we try to impress others with our piety. It does mean that we live our lives with such openness and transparency that others are able to see us turning to Jesus for help at that point in our lives when we need help most. When we are down and out, whipped and beaten by life's circumstances, we do not have to pretend that we haven't any problems and that everything is all right when in reality it is not. Instead, we can allow the very things that threaten to defeat us drive us into our Lord's everlasting arms. Whenever we are on top of things and everything is going our way, we do not have to try to grab all the glory for ourselves either. Let us be eager to look to Jesus for help when we need it and give him the glory and the credit due him when he helps us. Let us seize every opportunity that affords itself to offer thanksgiving and praise to his holy name.

Paul advised the Colossian Christians, "Whatever you do, whether in word or deed, do it all in the name of the Lord Jesus, giving thanks to God the Father through him" (Col. 3:17). To say and do everything in Jesus' name means to have our thoughts and activities saturated with the name that is above all names. It means that whenever we are doing the most trivial task for the least important of God's children, we will do it with the same amount of enthusiasm that we would express if we were doing it for the Lord. We will live our lives and fulfill our responsibilities day by day "as unto the Lord" and thereby glorify his name in our actions.

The reason the Christian writer writes, the singer sings, the preacher preaches, the teacher teaches and the cook cooks is to express his or her love for Jesus through the special talents, abilities, and interests that are uniquely his or hers. It is not primarily for public recognition, material gain, or personal fulfillment—although these may accompany the activity—but to glorify Jesus. Several years ago I went on a diet and over a period of six months lost thirty pounds. I had been struggling to lose weight for years. Once, I even resolved to go on a diet and ended up gaining ten pounds! But this time it was different. It was as if Jesus had taken me off in a corner and said to me, "You're going to lose some weight. You're going on a diet." And I said to him, "But Lord that's impossible. I've tried it before and it won't work. I can't do it without your help." His response was, "That's the whole point. You can't do it without my help. But you're going to do it and I will strengthen your will so that you can do it with my help." So, today I am thirty pounds lighter, and I could never have done it without Jesus. What reasons in your life do you have to praise the Lord? What does the Lord want you to do that you cannot accomplish without his help? If the Lord wants you to do something that will glorify his name, you can do it with his help.

Sharing in Worship and Fellowship

Our Lord once promised, "For where two or three come together in my name, there am I with them" (Matt. 18:20). We tend to underestimate the intensifying power of Jesus' name in a group context. But tremendous spiritual power is often expressed when the followers of Jesus come together and begin calling on his name. It was within the fellowship of believers that Simon Peter concluded concerning Jesus, "You are the Christ, the Son of the living God" (Matt. 16:16). In the presence of the other disciples Thomas had his doubts resolved and addressed the resurrected Jesus with the exclamation, "My Lord and my God!" (John 20:28). The power and authority to bind the forces of evil and set the captives free is expressed through the fellowship of believers and linked with the recognition of who Jesus is (Matt. 16:18–19). But most of the time Christians do not realize a fraction of their potential in Christ Jesus.

When the Gentiles found personal spiritual fulfillment in Jesus, Peter gave orders for them to be "baptized in the name of Jesus" (Acts 10:48) so that they could be officially identified with the church. To be baptized in the name of the Lord in the fullest sense is to have our minds saturated with and our consciousness flooded with the name of Jesus so that he is always in our thoughts and his spirit is always expressed in our actions and attitudes.

Whenever I look at the modern church I see those who have learned to call upon the name of the Lord and those who have not. Those who are consciously and unashamedly aware of the fact that they are serving in Jesus' name are expressing the full range of his power and influence in their lives. It is those who believe in his name, trust in his name, and call on his name who experience victory in Jesus. It is not those who call him Lord or Christ but those who know him as Jesus, their personal savior and constant companion, who are experiencing all that the Christian faith has to offer.

If we could only understand that the greatest power and authority in heaven or on earth is linked with the name of Jesus, then we would seek to overcome our reluctance to name the name that is above all names. People need to know that they can call upon the name of the Lord and be saved. They need to be told his name and taught how to use it. Sharing the name of Jesus with others is the secret of effective witnessing and successful evangelization.

Action Response

1. Look for specific opportunities to name the name of Jesus in conversation with others today. Try to do it casually and as a natural part of the conversation.

2. How did other people respond to your efforts? Why do you think they responded the way that they did?

3. How did you feel while doing this? Did you feel comfortable mentioning Jesus' name or was it a real struggle for you to do so?

5. Naming the Name for Others

Whenever the name of Jesus is exalted and glorified, the Holy Spirit is released and love, joy, peace, health, and healing are the inevitable result. Praying the name of Jesus for others allows the Lord to use our hearts, minds, and bodies as channels of his spiritual blessings. The most desperately needed, the least visible, and the most highly neglected ministry within the church today is the ministry of intercession. Our Lord said that his house would be called a house of prayer (Matt. 21:13). He continues to intercede for his people at the throne of grace even today. (Heb. 7:25). What we need as growing Christians, more than anything else, is to express the same spirit of prayer for others that our Lord expresses.

Sometimes we are frank enough to acknowledge this concern. We may even go so far as to promise to remember others in prayer. We may offer an occasional "God bless Mary or John" and thus fulfill our promise in a superficial manner. But seldom do we get down to the point where we actually do any serious praying for the needs of others. We allow other thoughts and activities to crowd out our best intentions. Perhaps what we need is an intercessory prayer focus that puts us in touch with the Master who prays for others continually. This is precisely the function that the name of Jesus can perform in our intercessory prayers.

Intercession in the Early Church

When the crippled man at the temple gate was healed through the prayer ministry of Peter and John, the people were astonished. As has been noted previously, Peter offered this simple explanation concerning the man's healing: "The God of Abraham, Isaac and Jacob, the God of our fathers, has glorified his servant Jesus. . . . By faith in the name of Jesus, this man whom you see and know was made strong. It is Jesus' name and the faith that comes through him that has given this complete healing to him, as you can all see" (Acts 3:13, 16). Whose faith was it that had healed the man? It certainly was not his own faith because no mention is made that he had ever heard of Jesus. He certainly did not know that Peter and John were disciples of Jesus. He was just hoping to receive a donation from them. It was Peter and John's faith in the power and authority of Jesus' name that enabled the healing power of Jesus to be expressed in the crippled man's life. Their faith focused in the mighty name of Jesus was used as a substitute for the crippled man's faith. The miracle of instantaneous healing was the result.

As much can be learned from reading whole books of the Bible as can be learned from studying in depth specific passages of scripture. As I study the book of Acts it becomes apparent to me that the name of Jesus was the focal point of spiritual power in the early church. The activity of the Holy Spirit seems to coincide with the frequency or infrequency with which his name was used. So important was the name of Jesus to those early Christians that when the Jewish religious leaders called the Apostles and warned them not to speak or teach at all in the name of Jesus, Peter refused to comply with their request (Acts 4:18–20). Later, the church met together and prayed for more boldness to share the name and asked for more miracles to be performed in the mighty name of Jesus. "Stretch out your hand to heal and perform miraculous signs and wonders through the name of your holy servant Jesus" (Acts 4:30). As a result the Bible records that "the place where they were meeting was shaken. And they were all filled with the Holy Spirit and spoke the word of God boldly" (Acts 4:31). The reason we are not praying more earthshaking prayers today and experiencing spiritual fulfillment in them so that we will become more highly motivated to proclaim God's word to a needy world may be that we have neglected to pray the name of Jesus on behalf of ourselves and others.

On the day of Pentecost, Peter said to the crowd of curiosity seekers that had gathered, "Therefore let all Israel be assured of this: God has made this Jesus, whom you crucified, both Lord and Christ" (Acts 2:36). When the leaders of the early church affirmed that Jesus Christ is Lord, their emphasis was upon the historical personality of Jesus who had come, lived and taught, died and arose from the dead, and performed miracles in their very midst. They were saying that Jesus of Nazareth is the Christ—the Messiah. He is the Lord of the universe—the divine logos through whom all things were created. Jesus of Nazareth is the son of God in a way that no other person has ever been or could be. He is the author of life and our only hope for eternal salvation and deliverance from sin and death.

In the book of James we find practical advice for daily Christian living. But even in the pages of this book we find the name of our Lord associated with faith and prayer on behalf of others.

> Is any one of you sick? He should call the elders of the church to pray over him and anoint him with oil in the name of the Lord.
> And the prayer offered in faith will make the sick person well; the Lord will raise him up. If he has sinned, he will be forgiven.
>
> —James 5:14–15

Effective prayer originates at the throne of grace, in the heart of the master intercessor and is channeled through our hearts and minds on behalf of others. It is the name of Jesus which gives such prayers their most effective focus so that they can result in healing and wholeness.

Jesus himself interceded for the needs of his followers prior to his arrest, trial, and crucifixion. In a portion of that prayer in the garden which he offered for them he prayed,

"Holy Father, protect them by the power of your name—the name you gave me—so that they may be one as we are one. While I was with them, I protected them and kept them safe by that name you gave me" (John 17:11–12). There is protection and safety in the name of Jesus because his name reminds us that Jesus is always with us. This does not mean that we will never experience pain, frustration, failure, heartache, sickness, or disease. It does not guarantee us a trouble-free existence or assure us of peace and prosperity. It does not mean that we will always be popular or that others will admire us. But it does mean that our faith in Jesus will be so strong that it will carry us through whatever circumstances life thrusts upon us. Because Jesus is with us, we will have the power to cope with life. Our faith will not be diminished by frustrating circumstances; it will be strengthened by them. In times of tragedy and disappointment, some people turn away from God and begin to see God as their enemy. "Why did God let this happen to me?" they often ask themselves and others. But because Jesus is always with us, our difficulties may instead move us deeper into our heavenly Father's embrace. That is the nature of the security, protection, and victory which we experience in Jesus' name.

Some Practical Suggestions

Allow me to offer a few practical sugges-
tions for naming the name of Jesus for others:

Affirmation: We can pray a prayer of
authority in which we affirm the fact that Jesus
is with the person in need and has the power to
help that person. Simon Peter used this type of
prayer when he prayed for the healing of a man
who had been paralyzed and confined to a bed for
eight years. "Aeneas, Jesus Christ heals you,"
Simon Peter triumphantly announced (Acts
9:34). Then he told the crippled man to get up
and make his bed because he was no longer sick.
And the man did exactly that!

Command: This kind of prayer has several
variations because in Jesus' name we have the
power and authority to command the sick
person, the affliction itself, or the oppressive
powers of darkness, as the situation demands
and the Lord guides us. Jesus commanded the
disease when he rebuked the fever in Peter's
mother-in-law. He commanded the afflicted
parts of the body when he told blind eyes to see,
deaf ears to be opened, and silent tongues to be
loosed. He commanded the afflicted person
when he told the lame to walk and the dead to
rise. He commanded the powers of darkness to
depart from the demon possessed and described

the woman with a bent back as having been bound by satan (Luke 13:16)—indicating that her particular physical affliction had its origin in spiritual bondage. There are no hard and fast procedural rules in these matters, and we really should not expect any. Jesus seems to have custom-tailored his prayers for healing to the needs of the individual. As the Spirit leads us, we should do likewise. What really matters is that we bring the power and authority of Jesus' name into focus upon the particular situation.

The Name Itself: Missionary and prayer warrior Frank Laubach offers the following strategy for intercession in *Prayer: The Mightiest Force in the World:*

> If you feel you have cheated yourself in the past by not having a technique in prayer, and if you wish to discipline yourself to this form of prayer, it is simple—so simple that a child can do it. You may say silently with each breath, "Jesus," while you look at the people you meet, trying to help Him reach them. If you think of something else important enough, say it, but if not, the word "Jesus" with every breath is enough. There will never be a more blessed, higher thought to broadcast over the world.

The Reality Visualized: Much has been reported in recent years concerning the value of creative visualization as a form of therapy for use with cancer patients. Leslie D. Weatherhead and other spiritual explorers have suggested a visionary means of channeling the reality of Jesus into the lives of those who need him. First, we should get a picture of Jesus in our minds, perhaps a favorite portrait or painting that we have seen. Then, we picture in Jesus' presence the persons for whom we are praying. We visualize them talking with each other. We see Jesus taking them in his arms and comforting them or placing his hands on the afflicted part of their bodies so that they will be healed. Finally, we picture them in our mind growing stronger and stronger until they become whole persons in body, mind, and spirit in Jesus' presence.

To pray in this way may seem like watching a beautiful movie unfold in your imagination. But such visionary prayers can produce tangible results. I have had the experience of praying for people in this unique manner and discovering that they were healed almost immediately or that their physical condition was greatly improved at the very hour that I prayed for them. One member of my congregation suffered a massive coronary in the middle of the night.

After talking with the family I immediately notified a number of people to start praying for him. While I was praying for him, a vision came into my mind of Jesus in the room with him, placing his hands over his chest. There was a brilliant glow coming from the sick man's chest. It almost looked as if Jesus were warming his hands over a fire in the man's heart. And I knew in that moment that the man would recover. The next morning the family reported that the doctors had said he was in critical condition but that he started getting better at approximately three-thirty in the morning. That was exactly the time that I had been praying for him and experienced my inner vision.

The Conversational Method: Finally, we can experience the freedom to talk with Jesus directly about the needs of others. We may want to say something like this: "Lord Jesus, one whom you love is in great need. Your love for her is greater than my own. Your knowledge of her situation far surpasses my own. You can do more for her than I can. Therefore, do what you will and can do to bring about her healing and wholeness, so that your kingdom might come and your name be glorified in her life."

By naming the name of Jesus on behalf of others we are seeking to create the most favorable conditions for them to touch Jesus and be touched by him. How they respond is still left up to them. We are simply *doing our part* by opening up a spiritual channel that would otherwise be closed. The rest is between them and the Lord. It is not a highly visible ministry, but it is certainly a greatly needed one. Once we have learned to pray the name of Jesus for ourselves, we are compelled to pray the name for others.

Action Response

1. Try silently praying the name of Jesus concerning every person that you meet or think of today in the manner described by Frank Laubach. What were the results? Did it make a difference in your life? If so, describe how it made a difference and what it was. Do you think that it made a difference in the lives of those for whom you prayed?

2. The next time that you need to pray for someone's healing, try the visual method of prayer described in this chapter. Was it difficult to visualize Jesus and/or the person for whom you prayed? If so, why? How did this prayer make a difference in your life or the life of the person in need?

3. When someone asks you to pray for him or her, try praying an assertive prayer. Say something like this: "In the name of Jesus of Nazareth, be healed of your infirmity." Or, "In the name of Jesus, receive the miracle that God wants to give you." Do you think that this manner of praying helped the other person or changed his or her situation?

A Prayer of Centering

We experience what we express. A faith that goes unexpressed will eventually wither and die. Pray this suggested prayer of centering often. You will be delighted to discover that as you use it, your spiritual sensitivity will be enhanced, and your outlook will be elevated. You will begin to experience the love, praise, thanks, and desire to be with Jesus that you have affirmed in such a manner that the entire spiritual climate of your life will be changed for the better.

> I love you, Jesus.
> I praise you, Jesus.
> I thank you, Jesus.
> I want to be with you, Jesus.
> Now and always!

Robert V. Dodd was born in Shelby, North Carolina, and is an ordained minister in the Western North Carolina Conference of the United Methodist Church. He received his A.B. degree from High Point College and his Master of Divinity degree from the Divinity School at Duke University. He has served churches in Cashiers, Lenoir, and Gibsonville, North Carolina, and is currently serving as pastor of Stanley United Methodist Church in Stanley, North Carolina.

The author has contributed many devotional articles to religious publications and has also written five previously published books: *Faith Is for Sharing, The Work of the Holy Spirit, Speck of Sawdust in My Eye, Your Church's Ministry of Prayer,* and *Helping Children Cope with Death.*

He conducts seminars and retreats related to spiritual formation and has always been an advocate of the value of prayer.

The author also enjoys family activities, jogging, swimming, photography, and traveling. He and his wife Ann have two sons, Justin Robert and Aaron Lewis.